The Dream and The Flowers

A Collection of
Traditional Style Verse
in
Standard English
and
Dialect

by Peter Foster

First published by
Words are Life
2021
www.wordsarelife.co.uk

First published in Great Britain in 2021 by
Words are Life
10 Chester Place,
Adlington, Chorley, PR6 9RP
wordsarelife@mail.com
www.wordsarelife.co.uk

Electronic version and paperback versions available for purchase on Amazon.

Words are Life is the new name for Scott Martin Productions.

Contents

Land

Inspired by the view of Pendle Hill.

Mile after mile of open land,
Farm land.
There's power in the land,
Power in the soil.

We salute our homeland.

We feed from the land:
from the plains and
The vales and the dales;

Or high wide moor,
Where landscape
Becomes escape.

But power ebbs from the land.
Our food?
From other lands,
Someone else's land,
Someone else's hungry land.

And someone else is hungry.

3 CINQUAINS

Sun

Sun
Life giving, lighting,
Burning, blistering, blinding:
Vital star of heaven.
Sun.

Shark

Shark,
Powerful, predacious,
Silent, stealthy, sinister,
Fearing not even man:
Shark.

Cat

Cat,
Feline, friendly?
Slinky, solitary, sly;
A creature that manipulates:
Cat.

A Boggart in Blackpool

I am an owd boggart, tha' knows
Tha' might see me wheer ever tha' goes
If I'm ceawr't on a post
Tha' maun't think I'm a ghost,
'Cause I'm NOT! I'm a boggart tha' knows.

Aw goo abeawt freetnin't'o week
Its drunk an' t' befuddled Aw seek,
For I am t' bein'
Fowk's frittened o' seein'
When they bob behint th' 'edge for a leak.

But freetnin's neaw not what it wus
Aw think as that is because
Life gooin' too fast
Fowk go wizzin' past
On a train, in a car, er on t' bus

Aw decided t' tek a vacation.
But wheer in all of this nation
Con owd boggart goo?
Aw thowt Aw know! Blackpoo'!
Just in time for th' illuminations.

Well Aw set mesell off straight fer theer
An' manifested on th' end o' t' north pier
Aw gi' a seagull a poke
It flew off wi' a squawk,
Then Aw felt summat plop I' me ear.
Aw' shouted, "tha great mucky brid!

Tha'll pay fer what tha' just did".
Then o its fithers dropped eaut
An' it fell wi' a skreaawk
An' steartled a slumberin' squid

Aw thowt up t' tower is where Aw mun be
As a boggart that's easy fer me;
Aw thowt in't it grand:
Wi' t' prom' an' t' sand,
An' t' piers strechin' aewt into t' sea.

Then fer some mischief Aw started to look,
So a hoss fray its caert Aw unhooked.
O t' passengers muttered,
An' t' driver he stuttered,
When th'oss trotted off, slung its hook

Aw'd 'eared t' Tower Ballroom looked good
There'd be freetnin theer, aye there would;
Aw went theer one neet
Bur it were me as took freet
Aw bumped into Craig Revel Horwood!

Aw went a bit further deawn road
Till Aw geet t' Madam Tussaud's
A sign said they'd gorra
Chamber of Horror;
But they were aw nobbut wax' warra fraud!

They'd, Frankenstein's monster, Dracula too;
Aw squat down behint 'em,then aw went "BOO!"
Ee t' fowk didn't haelf run,
By crin that were fun.
Aw thowt now warrelse conna do?

Aw drifted on down t' t' south shore
An' a fair ground wi' freetnins galore
Fowk go to be frittened
Or else be cawed chicken.
How could an owd boggart want more?

Aw spotted a sign as said "Ghost Train",
Tha' con imagine as to how I were fain
Aw went in to see
If there were owt theer like me,
But it were o decidedly tame.

Little black trucks as go up, down an' round
Through an eerie black tunnel an' it cost thi' three pound!
They fritten o t' riders
Wi' skeletons an' spiders
An' ghostly ethereal sounds.

A couple came in an' 'twas clear
As t' young lass were showin' some fear.
Aw thowt now for some fun,
So Aw tickled her bum,
Then hoo slapped him an; said "Joe, not 'ere!"

Naew Blackpoo's awreet fer some
Wi its tower, its piers an' its prom,
But Aw belong t' t' farms,
T' th'owd lanes an' barns,
So Aw reckon Aw'll be pikin' off whoam.

A Word

Is one word enough for a beginning?
And if it were, how long should it be?
How many letters should it have?
Is it conceivable that it would have only three?

Is one word enough for a beginning?
Can one word stand for all?
Could the word be heard with no one there?
How many tongues does it take to make a call?

Is one word enough for a beginning?
Can one word start a trend?
If one word was how it all began,
How many words will signal the end?

A Becalmed Atlantic Dawn

Another night of stillness
Ends with stillness
Still.
On a tall ship,
North of the line,
Sails hang
Like spiritless spectres.
The Atlantic sleeps
Deep.

Earth eases round
Another notch.
Bustling bazaars
Fall silent
In the heat,
Lulled by the rhythm
Of the Indian Ocean beat
As from Bombay's searing noon
A spear of light is hurled.

It strikes a lifeless mast
West of the Greenwich line,
Snuffs out Mars like a light,
Leaving, above and below,
Nothing but blue,
Deep, deep blue.

Haiku

River

Life-giving water
Or a devastating flood,
Contrary river

Wheat

Shimmering, verdant
Waving golden, ripening.
Soft white under brown.

Storm

Wild westerly wind,
Splintering, shattering crash;
Vacant woodland plot.

Earthquake

Thunderous riving
Masonry plummeting, crash!
Once firm earth shifting.

Homecoming

Transcontinental
Navigation miracle:
The swallows' return.

The Glorious Twelfth

This can be sung to the tune of
"The Hippopotamus Song"
by Flanders and Swan.

A sweet little red grouse was dust-bathing one day
On a heather-clad Bowland fell.
When green wellies and spaniels came traipsing her way
Just as her mother did tell.
They beat at the heather with sticks and they yelled
To frighten the birds into flight.
This poor little red grouse
In the midst of her de-louse
Said, "bloody hell something's not right!"

Chorus
On the twelfth, twelfth the glorious twelfth
Nothing quite like it for flaunting your wealth
Having some good fun
With a twin barrelled shotgun
That's how hunting is done
Without any stealth.

Northern moorland in August is the place to be
To witness the gentry at play;
Their affluence aplenty for all to see
As the innocent grouse they do slay.
They count up the bag at the end of the drive
And think their selves ever so swell.
They celebrate the slaughter
With Champagne and porter
Then calmly move to the next fell.

Chorus

Fly Lagapus lagapus, fly wild and free,
Although you're scared out of your wits.
Just think of your brethren for tomorrow they'll be
Served up for lunch at the Ritz.
The landed have handed you a fate that's to be
A target for their sport and fun;
They find it delightful
And not at all spiteful
To blast you with a twelve-bore shotgun.

Chorus

With a whirr of her wings she took to the air,
Taking care to fly close to the ground.
Then from up ahead on the fell-side somewhere
There came a spine-chilling sound.
The hunters they let off both barrels: BANG BANG!
She knew then that danger was nigh.
She drove hell for leather
Deep into the heather (he-he-he)
And smiled as the beaters passed by

Chorus

Original idea and chorus by Frank Gibson.

Memories

Images fray life, frozzen i' time.
Action replays in thi mind
No fast forrad nobbut rewind,
Images fray, life frozzen i' time.

A phrase fray a poem, a line fray a song
Ull trigger a thowt as tha' thowt were gone
Some's a bit hazy, others reight strong
Some are fleeting, yet some are life-long.

O t' youthful marlocks and distractions:
O t' fads an' t' music an' t' fashions,
O t'dances an' t' sweethearts an' t' passion,
Or t' days when meyt were on ration.

Edited, uploaded, saved an' ready to share,
O'er a pint err a brew err just sat in t' chair
Good uns an' bad uns aw filed wi' great care,
Do Aw get ony likes? Aye, but bod one err two to be fair.

Ah don't need clouds, Ah've getten me own store
Year after year adds to t' score.
Now there's poast-it notes on t' fridge door;
What did Ah come in t' bedroom for?

Memories are treasures of t' soul,
Oranges and lemons in life's fruit bowl
Awaiting a spark that prompts a recall
Memories are treasures of t' soul.

Bremetennacum Veteranarum

Bremetennacum Veteranarum town,
Wheer owd Roman sowgiers enjoyed well-earned rest.
They'd fowt fer th' Empire an' now laid weapons down.
At Bremetennacum Veteranarum town,
Or Ribchester, for that is now the modern noun.
Th' owd emperor towd em, 'lads, yo mun be my guests'
At Bremetennacum Veteranarum town
Wheer owd Roman sowgiers enjoyed well-earned rest.

2 Pieces of short verse

Marilyn

Norma Jean her real name,
Her looks and curves they brought her fame,
And a risqué pic when the wind did blow
Showed the world Marilyn Monroe.

Dragonfly

Dragonfly, oh dragonfly
How eratically you fly
It seems to me you could be
A dragonfly that drank a flagon dry

Moorland

High, wide, windswept places,
Home to curlew, grouse and plover,
Once devoid of human faces,
High, wide, windswept places,
Now people flock to open spaces
With children, spouse or lover,
High, wide, windswept places,
Home to curlew, grouse and plover.

A Manchester Sonnet

One Lancashire morn in eighteen nineteen,
When fooak were fere clemmed as meyt were so dear,
In St Peter's field a gath'rin wer seen,
So t' magistrates sent t' yeomanry theer.
These fooak bod axed fer fere prices an' wages,
An' claimed a reight to a voice an' a vote;
But thar't pown to find 'em in hist'ry's pages,
For its t' winners who write hist'ry, please note.
Orator Hunt cawed for peace, Halton for hussars.
The petitioners tried to stand their ground,
And mony on 'em hed to bear the scaers;
While fray sabre slash an' shot t' deead lay o round.
Wey mun remember Peterloo today,
Else haerd won reights mut be tekken away.

Plough Time

Dragging, down turning days,
Raindrops rattle on cab windows.
A landscape of stubble stretches out
Another farming year
Begins its final throes.

The engine revs,
The lever's lowered
The silver bladed share bites
Deep.

Earth has turned full circle,
Now we turn the earth,
Time for soil to sleep.

Yearnin' Fer Th' Ow Days

Some fooak yearn fer th' owd days
Fer t' seawnds an' t' seets an' t' smells
Like t'smook an' t' clatterin' o' steam trains
As took us to sea-side hotels.

Some fooak yearn fer th' owd days
Fer t' bobby ridin' along on 'is bike,
Kids playing footbaw an skippin' i' t' street,
'Op-scotch an' leap-frog an' t' like.

Some fooak yearn fer th' owd days,
Saturda' neet; off to t' flicks,
Or p'raps gooin' dancin' to t' palais
Is weer tha went for thi kicks.

Some fooak yearn fer th' owd days
In t' coffee bar, jivin' to Cliff an' the Shads
Young lads an' lassies flirtin' an' coortin'
Away fray their mothers and dads.

Some fooak yearn fer th' owd days,
When a phone sat on t' table i' th' 'all;
Or tha could tek four pennies to t' phone box on t' corner
But tha bod geet three minutes, that's o'.

Some fooak yearn fer th' owd days
Say kids 'ave it easy these days;
But we've fowt an we've an' striven fer mony a year
To do things i' better ways

Some fooak yearn fer th' owd days,
But th' owd days were poverty an' toil;
Tha worked like a foo long hours fer low pay
Until tha were dropped into t' soil.

Some fooak yearn fer th' owd days,
But fooak way back when wanted change;
They wanted fair wages, safe work an' warm houses;
That shouldn't be too 'ard to arrange.

Some fooak yearn fer th' owd days,
But th' owd days were blighted by war;
Tens o' millions suffered an' deed;
An' what the hell war it aw for?

Some fooak yearn fer th' owd days,
But if they'd nobut face up to t' truth
It's not really th' owd days they yearn for,
Aw as they yearn for is youth.

Step On The Brakes

Step on the brakes.
Life's going too fast,
People call out aghast.
Let's go back to the past.

Back to the past
To manners and grace
To life at much slower pace;
When folk knew their place.

When folk knew their place
And houses were cold
And fifty was old
No, let the future unfold.

Let the future unfold
Don't stand in a trance
Grasp every chance,
Join in life's dance.

But for all our sakes
Don't step on the brakes.

Insatiable Cannon

Insatiable cannon,
You continue to dine
On a feast of humanity,
And for the wine,
A claret.
A claret so fine
Though not from the vines
But the veins of young soldiers
It seeps through the sand,
Out of sight,
Out of mind,
It stains not the hand
Five thousand miles distant
That signals the fatal command.

Tanka

A Japanese lyric poem of thirty-one syllables, in lines of five/seven/five/seven/seven syllables.

Snowfall

Winter's spirit leaves
a laminated landscape
softly over night
early risers share the guilt
defiling earth's new mantle.

The Gale

Like God's secateurs
the gale cuts through the forest
Weak and dead are pruned
by the scything westerly.
Now growth can begin anew.

Salmon

To her stream of birth
she's tracked the vast Atlantic.
A bright torpedo
leaping weirs triumphantly
to maternal sacrifice.

Golden Grains

Golden grains for human needs,
Everyone can eat their fill;
A hearty feast of swollen seeds.

Supplying fuel for daily needs,
And every Scottish whisky still.
Golden grains for human needs

Crunchy flakes, early morning feeds,
Manufactured in a gigantic mill,
A hearty feast of swollen seeds.

No room for flowers we call them weeds
And claim to let them grow would kill
Golden grains for human needs.

We work the land and hope it yields
A crop to compensate our skill;
A hearty feast of swollen seeds.

So farmer grow the grain, bank the proceeds,
Well, someone has to pay the bill;
Golden grains for human needs,
A hearty feast of swollen seeds.

Deluge

The mighty veins of Europe fill and flood
And over-night they turn from friend to foe;
All in their path are left no place to go.
They drench the plains that once ran red with blood
And wash the land where warring armies stood,
Fed by the rain and melting snow.
The people hurry from the fearsome flow
Of water running where the highways should.
In ancient times the flood would fertilise
By brining goodness from the mountain side
Laying it down upon the barren land,
But now because we must commercialise,
And pander to our egos and our pride,
We cannot see we merely build on sand.

Hunger in the Cradle

Just take a look at the world of man,
What do you see out there?
People pushed around from the Shawnee to the San,
That's what you see out there.
There's hunger in the cradle,
In the garden there is war.

Gold and silver in your hills we find,
Hey, you can't live there.
You've got to move out when we open up the mines.
Hey! You can't live there.
There's hunger in the cradle,
In the garden there is war.

Cane and cotton and men for sale
Hey, you can't live there:
Diamonds in the rocks and oil in the shale,
Hey! You can't live there.
There's hunger in the cradle,
In the garden there is war.

Palm and cattle and rubber and corn,
Hey, you can't live there.
Yeah, we know it's where you were born.
Hey! You can't live there.
There's hunger in the cradle
In the garden there is war.

The Pit Bull and Poodle

The pit bull and poodle sat down to doodle
And drew up a monstrous plan.
They found in the east a fearful beast,
So there to do battle they ran.

They drove their war wagon and toppled the dragon
And shouted out 'hip hip hooray'.
But the defeated successor to Nebuchadnezzar
Haunted them day after day.

Red

On the importation of steel from communist China.

There once was a dread
That our workers were red,
That's what we read:
Our workers were red.

So we opened our stall
To the world as a whole;
The world answered the call
To a corporate ball.

How does it feel?
Now they've done the deal
Does it appeal to you?
Now that our steel

Is
Red!

Survival

Life skills
etched in faces confused by a changing world.
Uneducated shrewdness,
ethnic strength and beauty.
Timeless,
fertile lifestyle,
continuity, family bonds,
Now
threatened by Western educated ignorance.

A civilised serpent
proffers an industrial apple
to display economic nakedness.

Despite the riches of Eden.

Concerto in Sea

An oceanic orchestra plays in time
With the Pacific pulse
While the conductor soars aloft:
Wide, white wings counting down the beat.
Below, deep down below,
An eerie, aquatic chorus reverberates,
And duets with the seabirds' cries.
The wind section plays full-part,
It sings through masts and rigging
To the rhythm of the driving, pounding spray;
A vast maritime ensemble in harmony.

The Old Violin

Strings, silent, sleeping; how barren the bow
Of the old violin that Granddad used to know.
A mere collection of wire and wood,
He never did dream that ever it could
Lie dormant for two generations;
Just left in extended hibernation.
Not really forgotten or even ignored
And ever so carefully packed up and stored.
Sometimes dusted and polished to shine;
Or maybe playfully plucked, Marvinesque
Around nineteen hundred and fifty nine.

Small fingers, searching, stretching; now potent the bow
Of the old violin that Granddad used to know.
An instrument by magic awakened,
Singing once more, no longer forsaken.
The spirit, released by a caress
To grant a parental wish no less.
As from the lamp of Aladdin it flies
And carries the notes way up to the skies,
Where if Granddad can hear he'll surely rejoice
To know his old fiddle has found a new voice.

Tom Guitar

Dedicated to the memory of Tom Braund:
a musician and friend.

1.

A family man
A music man
A guitar man
A good man

2.

He played music
Clear and true
Folk or rock
Jazz or blue
Latin beats
Or old time swing
All came smoothly
From the string
Taken too soon
No time to say
The words we wish
He could hear today.

3.

All too briefly
He touched our lives
But his spirit lives on
In our hearts
And in our music
But we must
Now say
Goodbye
To
Tom Guitar.

The Wars of the Roses

There is a fair county, a county that's grand
'Tween Cheshire, Yorkshire and owd Westmorland
Fray Rochdale to Blackpoo', fray t' Mersey to t' Duddon
That county is Lancashire, an' by 'eck it's a good un.

That parcel o' land that I've just defined,
Was once known as a proud Palatine.
We'd fend for ourselves baht favour or fear
An' stand up for t' county we howd very dear.

Red is the rose that thrives in our bower:
A handsome, winsome, stately flower, 'tis said
Young Henry Six picked it, said: 'This is for me!'
Then towd cousin Dick 'Its white un for thee'.

Battles, one after t' other o went wi' a swing,
As they fowt like hell o'er who should be king
Henry Tudor fotched up an' ended their fight
And t' Tudor Rose joined the red with the white.

But 'ere, up i' t' north, on booath sides o' th' hills
This rankle ran deep and needles us still.
But naew its bod banter, nobody gets 'ort
Its nobbut o'er cricket or summat o' sort.

Canal Fest 2016

This poem was inspired by Randal Mundy's Staleybridge Wakes. I've tried to do something similar concerning Chorley's own Canal Fest 2016; an event organised to celebrate 200 years since the opening of the Leeds – Liverpool Canal that turned out to be such a "rieght good do" we celebrated the 201st too. There was hope that it could become an annual event but the fates conspired against us. However we had 2 good years and this is what it was all about.

I' t' seventeen hunderds some thowt it best
If a watterway ran fray th'east to west.
I' t' county o' Lancashire somedy said:
We'll start it at Halsall, bi' t' Saracen's Yed."

Wi' t' Yankee war, an' spats o'er weer it ud run
It wer aboon fifty year afoor it geet done
Bur i' 1816 after aw th' ifs an' buts
They oppened up t' Leeds-Liverpool cut.

Afoor long t' railways started to grow
They med t' canal booats look terble slow.
When motors on t' t' rooads med their way
It seemed th' owd canal ud 'ed it's day.

But leisure fooak revived it at last,
And med it a heritage part o' Lancashire's past
I' 2016, two hunderd year sen it wer done,
Somedy said: "Hey, let's eh some fun!"

They set up shop at Botany Bay,
deawn bi t' Lock an' Quay
An' t' sun shone breet an' clear upon this jamboree.
Well t' fooak tornt up an' it warn't so long

Afoor aw t' place looked middlin' throng.

They'd booat trips along t' canal fer fooak,
fer very little charge
Or tha could go an' hevva look round
an owd workin' barge.
Canoes and kayaks were paddlin' along in t' sun,
An' narra' booats fray far and near tornt up to join in t' fun.

They'd a classic car display; vehicles fray t' past,
Polished an' gleamin' they were surely built to last.
Sunbeam, Austin, Hillman, names no longer sowd,
I passed me test in a Morris like that;
meks me feel rayther owd.

Fer t' childer they'd fair-ground rides,
an' a mocked-up owd-time omnibus
Drivin' aw round t' site wi' aw t' kids wavin' at us.
Some went to Puddle Town Pirates t' enjoy a bit o' play
I'll bet they were aw rieght powfagged
bi it geet t' th' end o' t' day.

There were craft staws wi' nick-knacks fooak ud med:
Jewellery, carvin's, an 'erbal pilla' fer thi bed.
Earrings an' beads, a bracelet or a ring,
Aw manner of ideas if tha' wanted a bit o' bling

An' they'd food staws of every kind:
Spicy curries, chips, burgers, hot dogs, pies,
owt as yo've i' mind,
Ice cream an' candy floss, wine an' beer too;
Hooam med jams an' pickles;
or tha could go an' hevva brew.

An' as fer entertainment,
well, tha really couldn't go wrong.
Performers of every stripe wi' stories, jokes an' song
Music an' merriment to keep thi spirits high
To purra smile on thi face an' fotch a gleam to thi eye.

Sid Calderbank were theer i' wesc'ot an' flat cap,
Regalin' fooak i' t' Lancashire twang;
a straight forrad sooart o' chap.
Ee an' warra memory that mon ez, a thowt 'e'd ne'er stop!
'is recitals about Lancashire fooak,
like Bobby Grundy an' 'is shop.

Graham an' Bernadette were theer,
they caw thersels "Trouble at t' Mill",
Wi' fooak songs o' coal and cotton
an' dear owd Pendle Hill
Graham strums on 'is guitar, Bernadette sings like lark
And their songs went ringin' out across that bustlin' park.

They even 'ed a samba band
wi' Brazillian an' African beats;
Playin' drums to their heart's content,
ee, mon, whar a treat,
They'd lassies dancin', dressed i' fithers,
an' aw but welly nowt,
An' t' lads i' th' audience stood theer, gawpin',
wishin' as they'd mowt.

When it geet tort neet t' creawds started to thin
Aw rememberin' whar a beltin' day it'd bin.
Th' organisers were suited an' aw,
an' one thing soon became clear:
As we'd aw ed a such a gradely day,
we'd do it agean next year.

Dark Winter Days

Descend dark winter days, your time is close I fear,
For equinox bows to let you in.
The harvest's gathered, the swallows have flown,
Dandelion and thistle are blown.
The air is chilled, the wind is thin;
Dark winter days, I feel you drawing near.

Descend dark winter days, I know you will not win;
For solstice will once more see
You in defeat and on the run,
While we rejoice for our saviour son.
We'll celebrate, and then we'll see
Those longer days will soon begin.

Descend dark winter days, I know you will not last
Your fleeting, sleeting reign will fly.
By Candlemass we'll hear the robin sing,
Heralding the birth of gestating spring.
But to conquer yet I know you'll try
With your fearsome eastern icy blast.

Be gone dark winter days your power is at an end.
For equinox again will come,
And as heaven's torch lights your retreat
Our tenebrous time will be complete.
Lighter and longer our days become,
Goodbye dark winter days, hello bright summer, old friend.

The Rhythm of the Twelve Bar Blues

From hearts of darkness a spirit arose,
Through cane and cotton where Mississippi flows;
There the plantations exacted their dues.
Listen to the rhythm of the twelve bar blues.

Iron road, iron hand; John Henry's ghost
South to north, coast to coast
White over black, light the fuse;
Listen to the rhythm of the twelve bar blues.

Dixie minstrel, Uncle Tom, old Jim Crow;
It ain't *all* necessarily so,
To know the truth, search for the clues,
Listen to the rhythm of the twelve bar blues.

Dancing, drinking, fighting on Beale
The crack of the gavel, the Parchman deal
The hurt and the pain, lost love and the booze,
Listen to the rhythm of the twelve bar blues.

There's a voodoo woman: a Cajun queen
Livin' on a bayou in New Orleans;
She's got black cat bones, she's got John Conqueroos
Listen to the rhytm of the twelve bar blues.

Spreading from the delta like the Mississippi heat
North to Chicago sire of the Mersey beat,
Motown, Stax, and those 'Blue Suede Shoes';
Listen to the rhythm of the twelve bar blues

A three-chord bridge from dark to light,
Spanning cultures, 'Mama, that's alright',
Let the drums beat out the news.
Listen to the rhythm of the twelve bar blues.

A rhythm to harmonise the theme
At the heart of Martin Luther's dream
A key for everyone to use,
Listen to the rhythm of the twelve bar blues.

The Dream and the Flowers

A generation born out of war,
raised with it ringing in our ears,
They called us the 'Baby Boomers';
Ration books and bomb sites part of our early years.
There had to be change.

It could be said the change started with the Beat:
Drop out, move with the groove and follow your dreams.
A fleeting, American bloom,
but seeds were set and dispersed.
And the Beat moved on.

The Beat moved on.
Art school beatniks heard the jazz, heard the blues:
Said this music's hip, we don't need a colour bar,
We're not afraid of the dark.

The Beat scared the old white guard, but school made it cool.
Then the world Rocked as it rolled around space.
The Boomers boomed, out loud:
'We aint gonna study war no more!'

An urban poet with a dust-bowl style
Told us *'Times They Are A Changing'*
And that answers were *'Blowin' in the Wind'*.
And we wanted to believe.

A man spoke of a dream, a dream of change,
A dream of harmony: no divide.
But dreamers are not well received.
If in doubt: Deuteronomy 13; go check it out.

The Beat emerged from a Cavern and Stones rolled
A shot! A dreamer died. A generation wept;
Vowed to keep the dream alive
And tear down the walls of division.

The beat moved on to the Parisian street,
"Down with the Bourgeoisie! Loose those chains!"
Left became right, Right became wrong
And the reactionaries – reacted.

Then turmoil in the East:
"COMMUNISM MUST BE DEFEATED!"
And San Francisco flowered:
Tripped out in the surf and the sun; and the spliffs.

–

Sneers and jeers drained the power from the flower,
Chicago, Brixton, Toxteth shattered the dream.
But still we wanted to believe,
And we cheered at the fall of the Wall.

A chance for a continent to unite;
Celebrate a common culture,
Stifle old doubts and fears and
Embrace a future of peace.

"What!" cried the old-guard.
"Island nation!"
"Empire!"
"Two world wars for this!"

The pernicious poisoning began.
The land became divided, unstable;
The roots could not hold.
The buds of harmony became infected,
could not fully bloom.

Briefly, the dream came to Uncle Sam
Who then awoke with a start and found:
Yes, it was only a dream; and while he had slept
The mycelium of hate spread through the land.

A net was cast, a web of ancient prejudice
That encompassed the Western world.
An ocean can divide, an ocean can unite;
But a web entangles and traps.

A recipe of complacency and fear
Blended with faux patriotism and bombast yielded
A dish of dissent against the status quo;
Mantras rang out: "Take back control", "Drain the swamp".

Thus did power purport to pass to the people
And the tail was led to believe it wagged the dog,
As from the box of Pandora the demons flew:
Leaving Hope barely able to survive.

Fear, distrust, lies and deceit prevail;
Compassion, empathy and respect grow ever weaker.
Now as I age I look back and ask with a sigh:
Why did the dream and the flowers have to die?

A Climate of Dissonance: A Dialogue

Youth
Lessons can wait, the planet cannot,
Everywhere now is becoming too hot,
And what have you done? Not one jot!
Except ruin it all, that's what.
Lessons can wait, the planet cannot.

Convention
Hush now child! You speak out of turn.
The ways of the world are not your concern.
You're so very young you've so much to learn,
Yet you stand there and say that the world's going to burn.
Hush now child; you speak out of turn

Youth
But I am the future, you are the past
And the world you've created I know cannot last.
The ice caps are melting way too fast;
And we'll have to deal with the die you've cast
For I am the future, you are the past.

Comvention
Attending school is where you should be
Not constantly berating me
Over plastic islands in the sea
Or the demise of an inconvenient tree,
Attending school is where you should be.

Youth

Lessons teach reasoning, science and maths,
You have created a dangerous behemoth;
Fire and flood destroy all in their path;
And that is the reason for our wrath.
Lessons teach reasoning, science and maths.

Convention

But there's business to run, goods to be made,
Crops to be grown and produce to trade,
Jobs to create, bills to be paid;
So forget this Extinction Rebellion brigade,
There's business to run, goods to be made.

Youth

But business sees only the bottom line,
You say sort that and all will be fine.
You deny or ignore all the obvious signs,
Such as wild fires and a rising water-line,
For business sees only the bottom line.

Convention

But Earth in the past has been cold and warm.
How can you know that ***we*** do the harm?
It's a natural cycle of tempest and calm,
There's really no need for all your alarm,
For Earth in the past has been cold and warm.

Youth

Youth ***will*** not be silenced, that much is clear,
Although our words you don't care to hear,
Our studies show that the end could be near.
Youth must act now and act without fear.
We ***will*** not be silenced, that much is clear.

A Poppy for John

For a brother I never knew.

John didn't fight, John didn't serve
But because of a war he is laid in a grave
He wasn't an objector, his conscience was clear
But because of a war he has paid very dear.
I wear a poppy for John

A four year old boy, second day at school,
New lessons, new pals, new rules.
Fearful, excited? We'll never know,
For this young life, and 37 more, never had chance to grow.
I wear a poppy for John

23 August 1944 two American planes
Liberator bombers, oh, the irony of that name,
Went out on a test flight in Lancashire skies,
Unaware of events that were to materialise.
I wear a poppy for John

O'er Ribble marshes clouds changed day into night
A storm was coming the pilots aborted their flight,
Their orders were to return to their base.
Sadly, for one this was not to be the case.
I wear a poppy for John

Coal black sky over Freckleton town,
Torrential rain came driving down.
Thunder, lightning, children scared.
Such a storm had never been heard.
I wear a poppy for John

Approaching their base from the north- west
The two young pilots tried their best
To battle the storm by now in full force,
Lt Manassero changed his course.
I wear a poppy for John

Lt Bloemendal wrestled controls, screamed for more power
As he tried to escape this deadly shower.
A sudden down draught, a lightning flash
The tail plane detached then a sickening crash.
I wear a poppy for John

The village school took the direct hit,
In seconds the leaking fuel was lit
And flames engulfed the infant class.
38 children breathed their last.
I wear a poppy for John.

On the 23 August 1944 a B24 Liberator bomber crashed into Freckleton village school, destroying the infant class and causing damage to surrounding houses and a café. The planes took off from nearby Warton USAF base at 10:30, the school clock stopped at 10:47. After the storm it was a beautiful summer's day.
In total 61 people died that day: 38 children, 2 teachers, 7 civilians, 4 RAF servicemen and 10 USAF servicemen including the pilot and crew of the stricken aircraft..

December Rose

Cresting a garden hedge, defying the cold
Is a tiny nugget of winter gold.
A December rose,
More precious than those
That bloom so fine
At a more appropriate time.

A summer-long fight
Striving towards the welcoming light;
Until in the approaching-Solstice-gloom
This gem finally now will bloom.
A rebellious rose, away with tradition;
"I'll darn well flower despite the conditions!"

If convention says you're getting too old,
Remember that nugget of winter gold.
Our paths are not mapped out by fate,
Note the phrase 'it's never too late.'
Keep that flower in your sight
And don't give in to the fading light.

About the Author

Peter is a retired dairy herdsman from Lancashire and apart from writing, his other interests include music, gardening and photography.

A special thank you must go to Lesley Atherton at *Words Are Life* publishing, for her help and encouragement in bringing this collection to publication.

If you enjoyed this book, you'll find more publications available from Words are Life at www.wordsarelife.co.uk and on Amazon.